COMMUNICATION

*First published in the United States
in 1992 by*

Gloucester Press Inc.
95 Madison Avenue
New York, NY 10016

Library of Congress
Cataloging-in-Publication Data

Burnie, David.
Communication / by David Burnie.
p.   cm. -- (Animal behavior)
Includes bibliographical
references and index.
Summary: Explores the reasons
for animal communication
and the methods used, such
as sound, scent, and sight.
ISBN 0-531-17312-7
1. Animal communication-
-Juvenile literature.
[1. Animal communication.]
I. Title. II. Series: Animal
behavior (New York, N.Y.)
QL776.B87   1992
591.59--dc20
91-31946   CIP   AC

Printed in Belgium

The author, David Burnie,
has written and edited
many books on natural
history and technology,
including three that have won
educational publishing awards.

The consultant, Steve Parker, has written
more than 50 books for children
on science and nature.

Design: David West
Children's Book Design
Designer: John Kelly
Editor: Jen Green
Consultant: Steve Parker
Researcher: Emma Krikler
Illustrator: Graham Austin

Photocredits
All pages apart from cover and
pages 5, 10, 15 top, 16 top, 16
bottom, 20 bottom, 18 and 25 are
from Bruce Coleman Limited;
cover and pages 10, 15 top, 16 top:
Planet Earth Pictures; page 5:
Worldwide Fund for Nature; page
16 bottom, 20 bottom: Frank Lane;
page 18: Oxford Scientific Films;
page 25: FLPA.

ANIMAL BEHAVIOR

COMMUNICATION

DAVID BURNIE

GLOUCESTER PRESS
New York · London · Toronto · Sydney

CONTENTS

INTRODUCTION

Communication means sending and receiving a message. For most animals, communication is central to survival. It enables them to find food, warn off enemies, pair up with a mate, and bring up young.

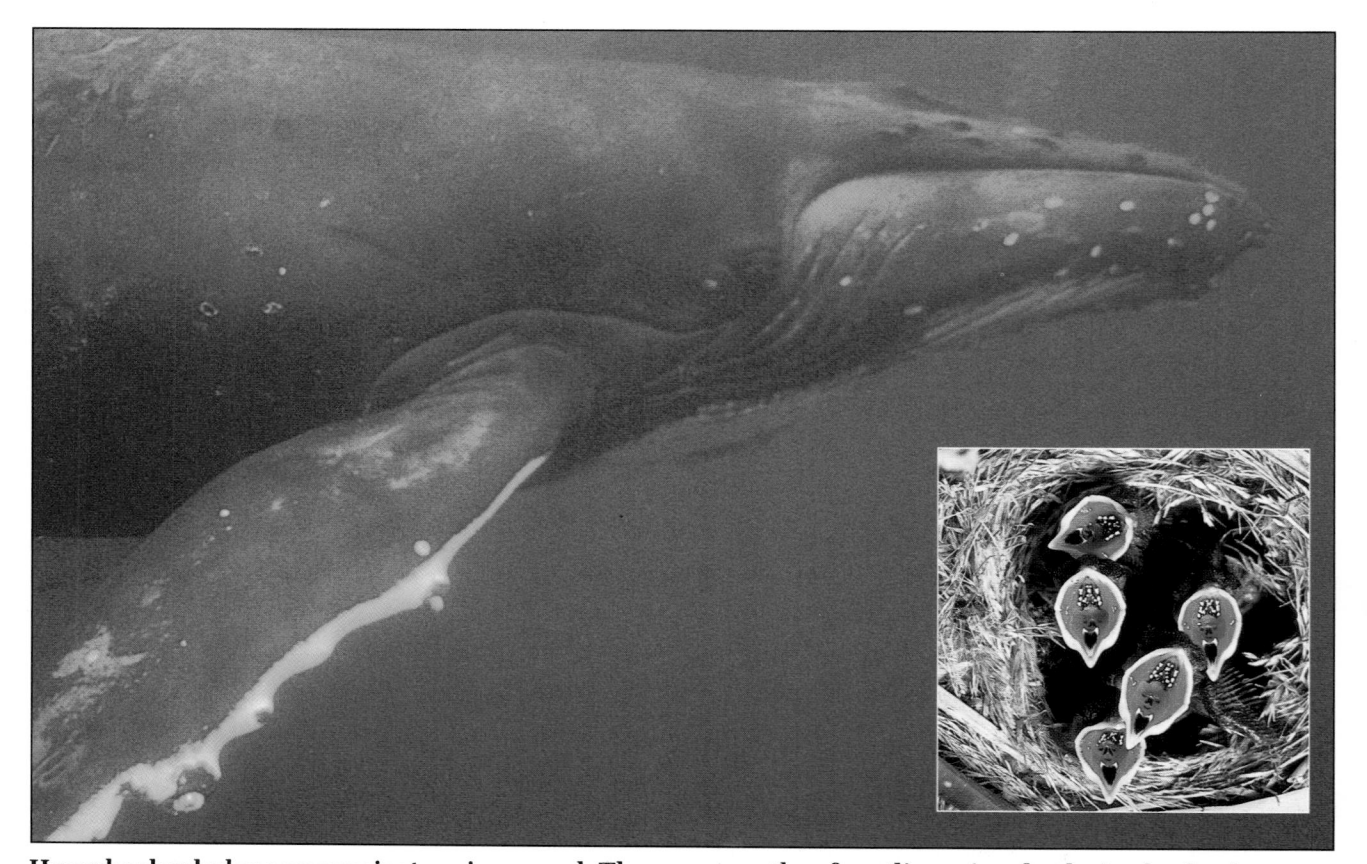

Humpback whales communicate using sound. The open mouths of nestlings signal a desire for food.

Humans communicate with each other in many ways. We use facial expressions to show if we are happy or sad. We use sound when we talk to each other, and touch when we hug or shake hands.

In nature, animals also communicate in many ways. They may communicate through sight, sound, smell, touch, or body language. For example, baby birds communicate with their parents through sight, sound and movement. A bearded tit nestling has bright colors on the inside of its mouth. When it wants food from a parent, it stretches up, opens its mouth and makes a cheeping sound.

Two kinds of communication
Much animal communication is between animals of the same species. This is often quite complicated, especially among birds and mammals. The eerie songs of great whales are an example.

Other forms of communication are between animals of different species. The messages sent here are usually simpler. In the deserts of North America, if a rattlesnake is cornered by another animal, it makes a loud rattling sound by shaking the loose scales on its tail. The sound warns that the snake is dangerous, and will attack if threatened further.

COLORS AND PATTERNS

Communication by sight (visual communication) is an important way of sending messages in nature. Colors and patterns can carry many different kinds of signals. Animals may show them off to impress their mates, or to frighten off rivals in the battle for partners.

A peacock's tail also carries a message. The tail feathers are long, and each is decorated with a beautiful "eye." When a peacock fans out his tail and displays it to a peahen, he is showing her that he is a fit and healthy male. A sickly male's tail feathers are in poor condition, and he does not spread and shimmer them so well. If a peacock's tail is impressive enough, the female may mate with him.

When the peacock displays to a female, the feathers at the base of his tail open into a fan. The peacock faces the hen and shakes his tail so that the feathers quiver.

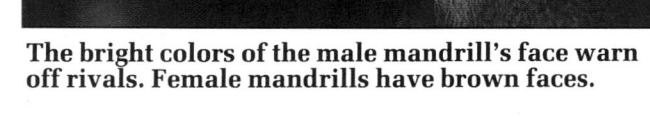

The bright colors of the male mandrill's face warn off rivals. Female mandrills have brown faces.

Facing up to others

The mandrill is a large monkey that lives in the tropical forests of West Africa. From a distance, the male's brown fur makes him difficult to see among the trees. But close up, his red and blue face is very striking. The mandrill's face is a form of communication. It tells other mandrills that he is male and that he is powerful and aggressive. This helps to establish his position in the group without a fight. Fighting carries the risk of injury, and many species of animals have developed ways of communicating to avoid it.

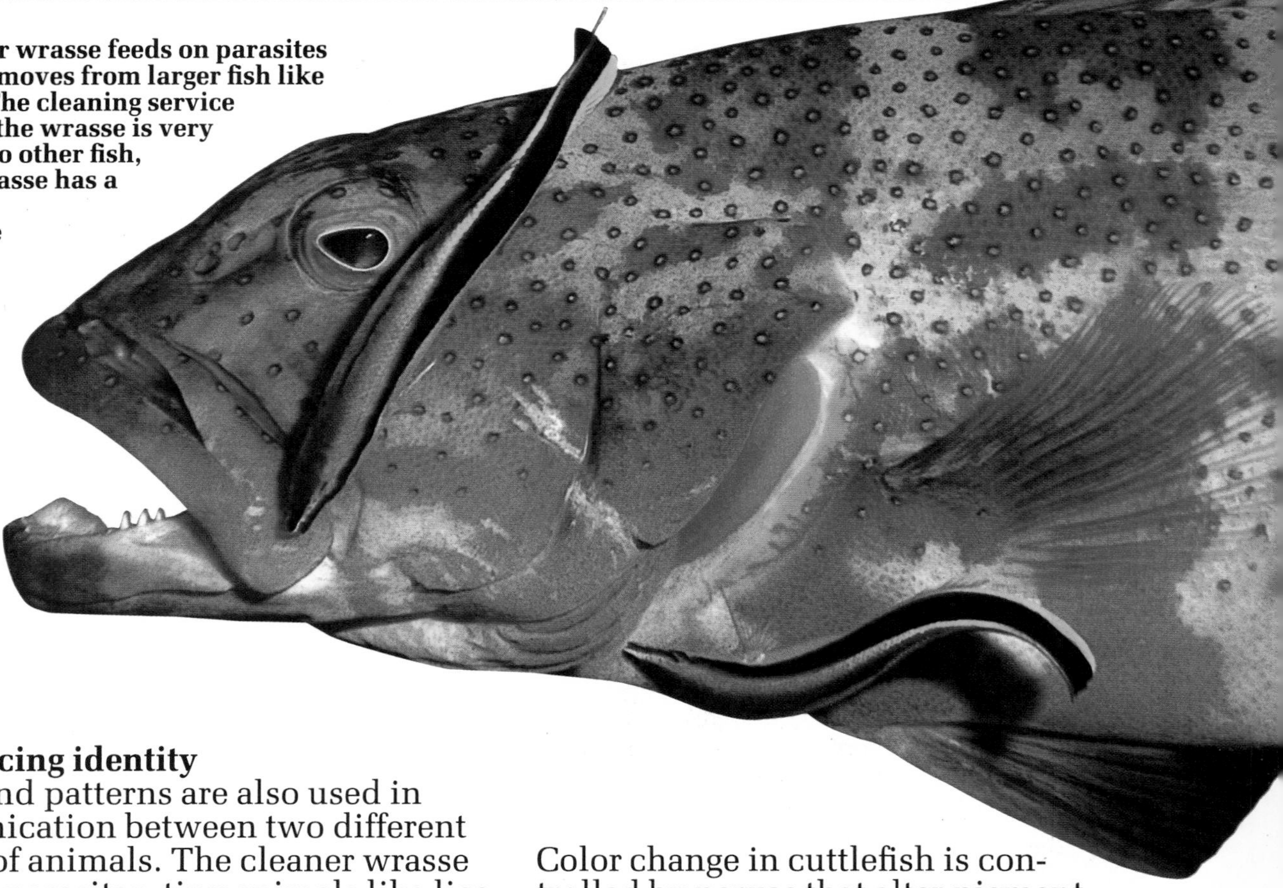

The cleaner wrasse feeds on parasites which it removes from larger fish like the trout. The cleaning service offered by the wrasse is very attractive to other fish, and the wrasse has a distinctive body stripe which advertises its identity to them.

Announcing identity

Colors and patterns are also used in communication between two different species of animals. The cleaner wrasse feeds on parasites, tiny animals like lice that infest other fish. These fish recognize the wrasse's stripe and the way it swims, and do not attack it. Sometimes they line up patiently and wait their turn to be cleaned.

For any form of animal communication to be effective, the species it is intended for must have senses which are tuned in to receive it. Bright colors and patterns would not be effective for communication between members of a species with very poor eyesight, such as moles! The good vision of birds, mammals and creatures like squid and cuttlefish is linked to their need to receive complex visual signals.

All change

Animals that change their color can communicate in a more complex way, sending a series of visual messages. Cuttlefish use the quick-changing colors and patterns of their bodies to communicate with others of their species. As waves of dark and light color ripple over their bodies, their appearance changes instantly.

Color change in cuttlefish is controlled by nerves that alter pigment (coloring) cells in the creature's skin. A male cuttle who is aggressive and ready to battle signals his intention by turning very dark all over. Scientists are still learning more about this complex, fast-changing communication.

If a cuttlefish is agitated or excited, waves of color move even faster over its body.

WARNINGS AND TRICKERY

Some animals use bright colors to send visual messages which warn that they are poisonous or taste nasty. Other animals imitate these colors, though they are not harmful or poisonous themselves.

Many stinging insects, such as bees and wasps, are colored yellow and black. These bold colors warn birds and other predators not to attack. Other insects, such as monarch butterflies, have poisonous flesh. They have bright warning colors, too.

Warning colors are a signal to all kinds of predators, from birds to lizards and mammals. Certain colors and patterns – spots or stripes of red, yellow, and black – are common to many animals, which reinforces the warning message. A predator that attacks a wasp, and gets stung, will be less likely to attack a bee with similar colors.

Some of the world's most deadly animals are the arrow-poison frogs of South America, which have poison glands in their skin. The frogs' brilliant colors warn other animals to keep away.

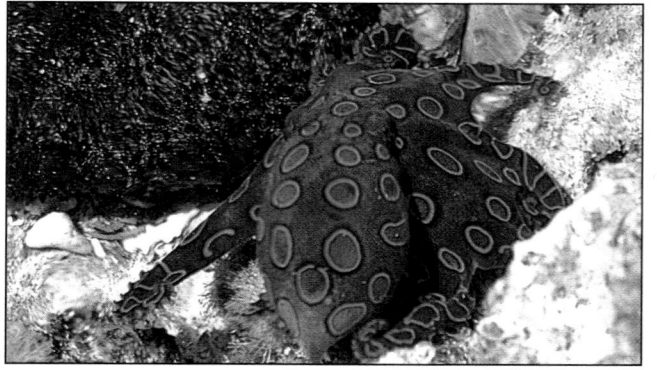

The blue-ringed octopus is only 12in long, but its bright rings warn that it has a fatal bite.

You have been warned!

Other warning colors are effective underwater. The blue-ringed octopus lives in Australasian waters. Its dull, mottled skin provides good camouflage against the rocky seabed. But when the octopus is threatened, blue rings appear in seconds all over its body, and glow like neon lights. The rings warn of the creature's deadly bite, which is so poisonous that it can kill a human.

It's a trick

Animal colors and patterns do not always tell the truth. Some species of moths, flies, and beetles look just like bees and wasps. Although these insects are quite harmless, they use the same yellow-and-black stripes to convince other animals not to attack them. This kind of deception is called mimicry, and is very common in nature.

The hoverfly's colors make it look like a wasp, but unlike the wasp, it has no sting.

Plain tiger monarch butterflies from Africa and Asia have orange-and-black colors that warn predators such as birds that their flesh is poisonous. Females of one species of diadem butterfly look almost identical to monarchs. Though their flesh is not poisonous, mimicry protects them.

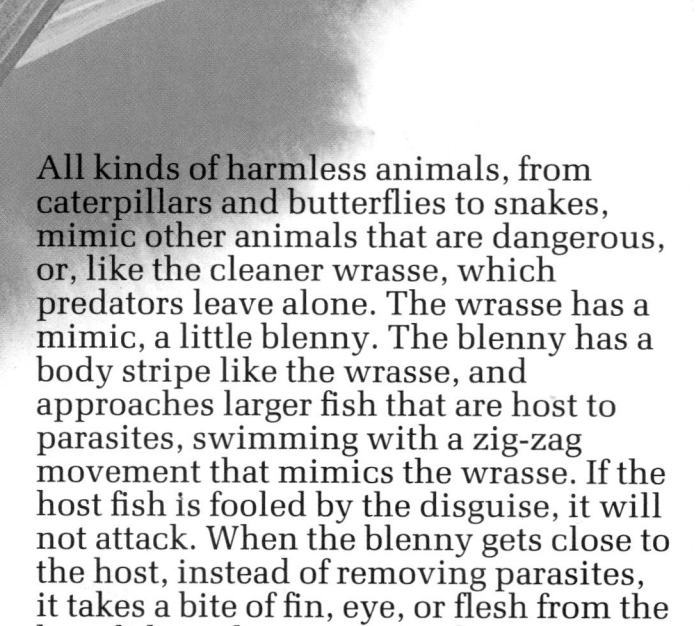

Plain tiger monarch

Diadem butterfly

All kinds of harmless animals, from caterpillars and butterflies to snakes, mimic other animals that are dangerous, or, like the cleaner wrasse, which predators leave alone. The wrasse has a mimic, a little blenny. The blenny has a body stripe like the wrasse, and approaches larger fish that are host to parasites, swimming with a zig-zag movement that mimics the wrasse. If the host fish is fooled by the disguise, it will not attack. When the blenny gets close to the host, instead of removing parasites, it takes a bite of fin, eye, or flesh from the host fish, and swims away fast!

LIVING LIGHTS

Some kinds of animals have organs in their bodies that produce light. When it is dark, they flash their lights on and off to signal to others of their species, or to lure prey toward them.

Flashlight fish create an eerie swirl of lights that blink in the darkness as the fish dart to and fro.

Lights in the water
When night falls over the Red Sea and Indian Ocean, tiny flashlight fish rise to the surface to feed. Each fish has a pair of "headlamps," one beneath each eye. The light is produced by bacteria that live there. Each fish has flaps of skin that it raises to cover the lights, and lowers again to make them flash on and off.

The flashlight fish uses its lights to communicate with its own species and to confuse predators. It communicates with other flashlight fish to avoid getting too close to them, so that the shoal is spread out evenly to feed. And if a flashlight is threatened by a predator, it swims away in a zig-zag path, flashing its light on and off very quickly to baffle the animal pursuing it.

Some fish also produce light in the blackness of the deep sea. Deep in the North Atlantic Ocean, the lanternfish has rows of light-making organs called photophores along its body. When lit up, the fish looks like a miniature jetliner at night. The lights may help it to identify other individuals in the shoal and find a partner, and they may also be used to confuse predators.

This South American firefly has two yellow lights on its back, and a third red one on its underside.

Some deep-sea fish use light to lure prey toward them. The deep-sea anglerfish lies on the sea floor, dangling a glowing "worm" above its mouth. Any animal that tries to nibble the lure is swallowed as the angler opens its mouth and sucks in whatever is near.

Lights on land

Certain land animals can also produce light. Such animals are nocturnal (active at night), and some have evolved signaling systems with their lights, for sending messages after dusk.

Fireflies are small beetles that live in many warmer parts of the world. They use light to attract a mate. After darkness falls in some parts of North America, female fireflies gather on the ground. The males fly overhead, flashing light from the undersides of their bodies. There are a number of species of firefly, and the males of each kind flash their own particular signal, like Morse code from a lantern. When a female recognizes the flashing code of her own species, she signals back to the male, and he lands beside her.

On land as in the sea, living lights can be deceptive. When they are hungry, some female fireflies lure the males of other species to them. They flash a response when these males signal overhead, but eat them when they land.

Larvae of fungus gnats glow in a cave in New Zealand, using light to lure prey toward them.

MAKING NOISES

Many species of animals use sound to communicate with one another. Some have powerful voices, and their roars and howls can be heard a long way off. Other animals have very different ways of making sound.

In tropical forests, visual signals are easy to miss in the tangle of trunks and leaves. Sound is a good way of communicating there, and forests are often filled with the voices of animals. Among the loudest of all forest calls is that of the red howler monkey of South America. Howlers feed on leaves and live in small groups, each with its own treetop territory. These monkeys use their large voice-boxes to produce a piercing cry which can travel over a mile, proclaiming ownership of a particular patch of forest.

Mating calls

Male animals of many species use their voices to attract mates or to impress rivals. During the mating or "rutting" season, the male elk makes a loud roaring noise. This is a challenge to other males and a signal to females that they should stay in his herd.

Red howler monkeys call each day at regular times. They listen to the howls of neighboring groups, to judge how many other groups are in the area and how close they are.

A male puddle frog croaks to attract females of his species. His call is amplified by twin throat sacs.

Some small animals can also produce loud noises. Many species of frog have baglike membranes connected to their mouths. These membranes fill up with air when the frogs croak. They vibrate like the skin of a drum, to amplify the sound (make it louder). Frog ears are tuned to the pitch of the croaks. They distinguish the calls of different species and even of individual frogs.

In flight, a female mosquito's wings produce a sound that the male can detect with his antennae.

Not all animals use their voices to make sound. We may recognize a high-pitched humming in the air as the sound of a female mosquito in flight. The noise is produced naturally by the rapid beats of the female's wings. For a male mosquito the sound has particular meaning. It tells him where the female is, and he can use it to find his way to her, even in complete darkness.

The male stripe-winged grasshopper has a special way of producing sound called stridulation.

Crickets and grasshoppers make noise by stridulating. Grasshoppers scrape their legs against their wing covers; crickets rub their forewings together. The song produced sounds to us like an almost continuous chirping, but is in fact broken up by short gaps, like rapid Morse code. Different species have their own codes. Males use them to attract females and warn off rival males.

SINGING A SONG

Birds are expert at communicating by sound. Nearly all birds make calls to identify themselves and attract a mate, to defend a territory and warn of danger. Some produce the sustained sequence of notes we call a song.

A familiar voice

Birds often use sound to identify each other. This is particularly important to those that nest in large groups, such as seabirds and penguins.

Gannets are seabirds that nest together on rocky cliffs or islands. To our eyes, the birds look almost identical. When a gannet returns to the colony, it has to find its mate among thousands of other birds. As it comes in to land, it makes a loud call to announce its arrival.

Its partner recognizes the call, and answers from the nest. It guides the approaching bird so that it lands in exactly the right spot.

In Antarctica, penguin parents and chicks find one another in the same way. A penguin parent returning with food must find its chick among thousands in the nursery. It calls out, and finds its way by listening for the chick's answering cry.

A gannet calls out to its mate in the nest site. Despite the volume of sound produced by so many birds, each gannet can pick out its partner's voice.

Many birds can produce a sequence of notes that rise and fall in pitch, sending a melodic signal we call a song. Each species of songbird has its own way of singing. A few birds, like the skylark, sing in flight; most, like the wren, sing from high perches, so that the sound carries a long way.

Every species of bird has its own type of song. Two species that appear almost identical visually, such as the chiffchaff and willow warbler, usually sound very different because they use their songs to tell each other apart.

The wren is a bird that lives close to ground level, but to sing, it flutters to the top of a bush or a small tree. For such a small bird, its song is astonishingly loud.

Female chiffchaffs find their way to males of their species by listening for the right tune.

Birds of the same species sing their tune in a slightly different way. The "accent" of a song varies, depending on where the singer lives. Studies on chaffinches showed that birds from neighboring valleys had different accents, learned from their parents.

Dawn chorus
Singing uses up a great deal of energy. Many birds sing loudly only twice a day, at dawn and dusk, to announce their ownership of a territory. Different species of birds sing at different times during the chorus. If a bird does not sing at its usual time, its neighbors notice and move into the unoccupied territory.

Starlings are good mimics. They can copy the songs of other birds, and even the ringing of a telephone.

SIGNALING BY SMELL

Sounds are effective for long-distance communication, while visual messages work well at close quarters. Smells can also be effective signals, particularly as they last for hours or even days after the sender has gone.

A picture in scent

Humans do not have a very good sense of smell, and sights and sounds tend to be more important to us. But many other kinds of animals rely a great deal on smell. A dog's nose is as important as its eyes for investigating the world around it, as you will know if you have ever taken one for a walk. By picking up traces of scent, a dog can tell what animals have passed by, and how long ago they were there.

Scent is made up of small amounts of chemicals produced by the body. All animals – including humans – give off a characteristic scent which lingers on the ground and in the air after they have passed. Animals with sensitive noses can detect the scent, and tell what kind of animal it came from.

On the African plains, male cheetahs mark trees with scent to show where their territories are.

By sniffing, a wolf can find out another's sex, breeding condition and where it has been.

Making a mark

Many mammals leave scent signals to communicate with others of their species. When a wolf, dog, or fox urinates, it leaves a "scent signpost" that tells others what sex and species it is. Many animals use scent to mark the borders of their territories. Male members of the cat family, from tigers to domestic cats, mark their territories by "spraying." They back toward an upright object and mark it with a strong-smelling form of urine.

Aye-ayes are mammals which live in trees in Madagascar. They wipe their urine over their feet, and leave the scent along the branches as they clamber about. Deer have scent glands just below their eyes. They rub their faces against grass stems, trees, and posts to leave their mark. The hippopotamus has an even more unusual way of leaving its scent signature: it scatters its dung with its tail as it walks along.

Aye-ayes leave trails of scented urine on branches. If moved, they quickly mark a new home.

The female atlas moth uses pheromones to signal to her mate. When the male's feathery antennae detect the faintest trace of the pheromone, he immediately flies toward its source.

Odors in the air

Some animals communicate by smell using substances called pheromones. These are chemicals that can be released into the air, and they are very powerful. Only a minute quantity needs to be released by one animal to attract another or change its behavior. The female silkworm moth uses pheromones to attract a mate. She releases a tiny puff of scent that the male can detect almost a mile away.

BODY LANGUAGE

Many animals communicate with others by the way they move or hold their bodies. Body language can be used to convey various messages, from aggression to playfulness or submission.

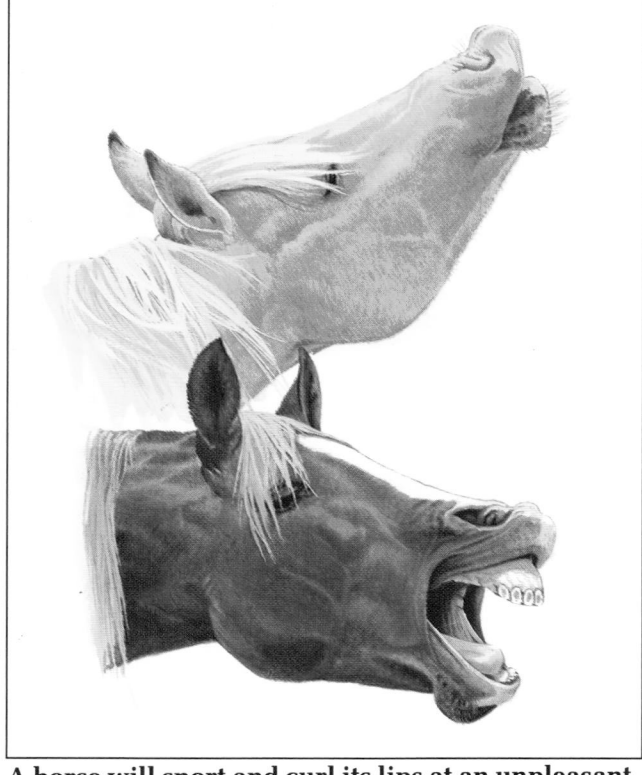

A horse will snort and curl its lips at an unpleasant smell. It bares its teeth when yawning.

A threatened swan hisses loudly and holds its wings half-open to make it look larger.

We can usually tell the mood of another person at a glance, by his or her facial expressions. Animals also have gestures and expressions. A horse can send various signals with its ears, tail, and body. In the wild, horses live in herds in open country. Body language is an effective means of communication for them, and humans have learned to recognize their signals because horses are very useful to us. A horse with its ears pricked and tail held high is excited. One with its ears back and tail held low is frightened. Many animals use body language to tell one another that they are relaxed, afraid, or angry.

Larger than life

Some animals use body language to communicate with animals of a different species. If a cat is cornered, it stretches up and arches its body. Its fur stands on end, and the animal makes a loud hissing sound. In this way the cat gives the impression of being bigger and more powerful than it really is. The swan responds with similar body language when threatened (above). The hiss is a warning signal common to cats, swans, geese, and snakes.

The Virginia opossum of North America plays dead to foil predators who only take live prey.

On the plains of Africa, Thomson's gazelle use body language to try to prevent predators like wild dogs from attacking them. When threatened, the gazelle leap vertically into the air. This display is called stotting, and through it each gazelle signals that it is fit and would probably escape if attacked.

Sometimes the signals animals send are even more misleading. If a Virginia opossum is threatened, the animal lies motionless and pretends to be dead. Many predators will not attack or eat animals that are already dead. Once the danger is over, the opossum "comes to life" and scampers off!

Keeping order

Many animals that live in packs use body language to communicate with others. In a pack of African wild dogs there is a strict chain of command. If a junior dog squabbles with a senior one, the senior dog will threaten it by raising its hair and showing its teeth.

But the senior dog does not often need to follow its threat with an attack. The junior dog responds with another body sign, called an appeasement or submission posture. It cringes low against the ground, making itself look small and unthreatening. These postures are seen in many animals that live in groups, from dogs and wolves to gulls, chickens and apes.

KEEPING IN TOUCH

Touch is an important way of communicating when animals are close together. Parent animals use touch to maintain contact with their young, and adults use it to send messages and keep together as a group.

A male white-handed gibbon grooms a female. Grooming is an important means of communication.

Mothers and young

Many animal parents and their young use touch to communicate with one another. Touch is a silent way of getting a message across, so it is very useful in emergencies. If danger threatens a family of wolf cubs, the mother wolf must convey her young to safety without attracting further attention. She picks up each cub in turn by the scruff of its neck. As soon as a cub feels its mother's mouth against its neck, it lets its body go limp. This allows the mother wolf to carry it more easily, so that the whole family can be moved to a safer place without being noticed by an enemy.

A mother wolf keeps a watchful eye out for danger as her cubs play together.

Lionesses keep in contact through touch, sleeping in a pile in the shade of a tree.

Displacement activity

Sometimes grooming provides a way of avoiding a fight. If two chimps get involved in a quarrel, they may suddenly begin to groom each other. Grooming calms the animals down without the need for either to admit defeat. This form of behavior is called displacement activity. It occurs when a creature suddenly stops what it is doing, and becomes involved in doing something entirely different, that appears to be out of place in the present situation.

Grooming and preening

Adult animals also communicate through touch. Many animals spend a lot of time grooming their fur or feathers to keep clean. Some animals communicate by grooming each other.

Chimpanzees may spend hours every day carefully searching through each other's fur, picking off fleas and lice that feed on blood. Grooming is a means of keeping in touch with relatives, and also shows who is in charge. When two chimps groom each other, the more senior always has its fur groomed first. The younger chimp shows its lower status in the group by giving the other animal first turn.

Ants live in colonies of many thousands. They spend a fifth of their time in the nest touching others. Mainly, they touch antennae in a kind of "nest recognition" signal. Intruding ants that do not know the "password" may be attacked. Ants also communicate about the location of food, about nest repairs, and even about the weather.

FOLLOW THE LEADER

For many animals, being part of a group is an important way of avoiding danger. There is safety in numbers in a herd or a shoal, but keeping together as a group involves constant communication and attentiveness.

Wildebeest live in herds many thousands strong. Running is their main way of escaping from danger.

Animals that live in groups stay together by keeping in touch with one another continually. On the open grasslands of Africa, wildebeest in herds communicate with each other by sight and sound. As they feed, these animals look around constantly. Being in a group means there are many pairs of eyes on the lookout for trouble. If one wildebeest sees a predator such as a lion approaching, it starts to run. It also grunts a warning. The other wildebeest recognize these signals and run to safety.

Ducklings follow their mother closely and make cheeping sounds to let her know where they are.

Are you my mother?

When a duckling hatches, the first thing it notices is usually its mother. The duckling learns to recognize her in a matter of minutes, and then follows wherever she goes. This is called imprinting. Scientists have discovered that when it breaks out of the shell, a duckling does not know instinctively what an adult duck looks like. Instead, it imprints on the first large moving object it notices. If the first animal it sees is a human or dog, the duckling will follow it as though it were the mother duck.

Safety in single file

Many animals obey the instinct to follow others of their species. The caterpillars of some moths form lines as they move from one foodplant to another. They keep in touch mainly by smell, following the scent trail laid by the leading caterpillar. Following one another cuts down the risk of being eaten if a predator is encountered, since the predator will eat the leading caterpillars, satisfy its hunger and allow the rest to continue unharmed.

In the Caribbean Sea spiny lobsters migrate in lines, keeping in contact by sight and touch.

Sometimes one species leads a different one. In Africa, the honeyguide bird has a particular call which signals the presence of honey. It uses the call to lead honey badgers to bees' nests. The bird knows that the honey badger will break open the nest to collect the honey. Afterward, the bird will be able to eat the bee grubs and the remains of the honey, as a reward for finding the nest.

A honeyguide bird shows a bees' nest to a honey badger. This relationship, in which two animals from different species help each other, is known as symbiosis. It is made possible by communication between the two species.

A COG IN THE MACHINE

Animals such as termites, ants, and bees live together in colonies made up of one very large family. Inside the nest, special kinds of communication make sure that the group functions efficiently.

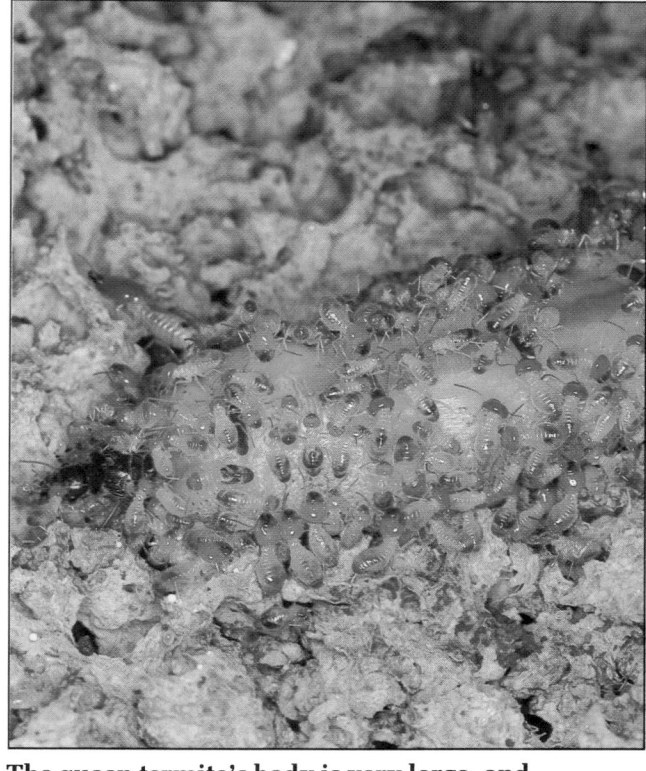

The queen termite's body is very large, and produces all the eggs needed for the colony to thrive.

A queen bee's pheromones control the work of the tens of thousands of bees that live in her hive. Her chemical signals ensure that food is collected, the young bees looked after, and the hive kept clean. The queen's pheromones also make sure that young queens in the hive are not raised except at specific times of the year.

If the queen is removed from the hive, the supply of her pheromones stops. The bees rush about in confusion, and then start to build special cells in which young queens will develop. Until a new queen is in charge, the hive cannot function normally.

Chemical communication

Deep inside a termite nest, the queen termite lives in a small chamber surrounded by guards. From her cell, the queen controls all the other termites in the nest. She communicates with them by releasing pheromones (see page 17). Pheromones are substances which are produced by one animal – often a queen termite, ant or bee – and passed on to others. Only minute amounts of them are needed to pass on the message. Sometimes pheromones waft through the air, but they can also be passed on in food or in special secretions that are spread by touch or footprints.

Worker bees surround the queen. They carry away the eggs she lays and place each in a cell of its own.

Dancing bees

As well as using pheromones, honeybees have a unique way of telling each other where food can be found. They do this by performing dances. Bees feed on nectar and pollen from flowers. When a bee finds a good source of food, it quickly returns to the hive. There it dances on the honeycomb, and is surrounded by the other bees. The smell of the flowers clings to the dancing bee, helping its nest-mates to find the food.

If the source of nectar is close, the bee performs a curving dance (left below). If the source is farther away, it dances a figure eight (right). The angle at which the bee travels on the comb in the middle of the figure is the same as the angle between the hive, the food and the sun.

Naked mole rats are the only mammals that live in colonies like those of bees and wasps.

Some species of mammals that live in colonies also use pheromones. Naked mole rats are bald and blind animals that live in small groups in underground burrows in Africa. Like honeybees, each group is ruled by a queen. She is the only member of the colony to have young, and her pheromones stop the other females from reproducing. Other adult mole rats dig burrows and bring food to the nest. In this way the work of producing young and finding food is divided efficiently within the group.

TAKE YOUR PARTNER

When animals come together to breed, they are often wary of each other. In many species, the two partners perform complicated dances and exchange special signals to form a bond before they mate.

The displays of the great crested grebe test out each other's stamina and awareness.

the pair dive underwater to collect weed in their beaks. Then they swim to the surface and paddle along furiously breast-to-breast. After testing their partner with weeks of these dances, the birds mate and raise a family.

Scorpions lock their pincers together and dance for hours before mating is completed.

Joining the dance

When many species of birds pair up for mating, they perform displays called courtship rituals. The displays of the great crested grebe are among the most elaborate in the bird world.

Great crested grebes have four distinct courtship dances. When the two birds meet, they perform the first dance, in which one bird dives underwater and then paddles on the surface with its body held upright. The second movement is a display of head shaking, and in the third, one of the birds rushes past its partner, splashing across the water. In the last and most spectacular dance,

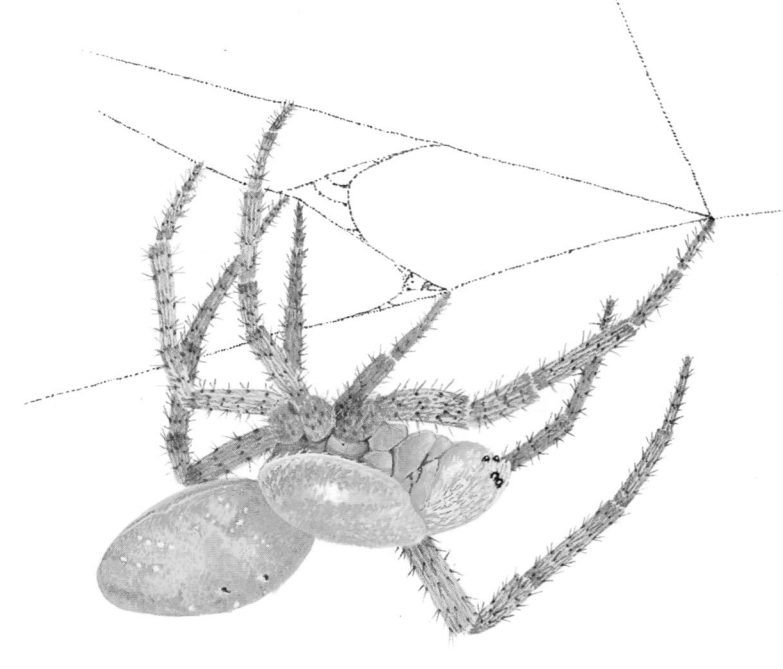

Avoiding being eaten

For male spiders, scorpions and other small animals, mating is a dangerous business. If the male is not careful, he may end up as a meal for his partner.

Male spiders are often much smaller than females. Before mating, the male orb-web spider approaches the female's web, and tugs rhythmically on its strands. His tugging causes a particular code of vibrations that tells the female not to attack him. Gradually, he inches forward until he meets her and they mate. But even then he is not safe. After mating, the female may still eat her partner before he has a chance to escape.

Other kinds of spiders, and some insects, have a different way of avoiding danger. In these species, the male offers the female a "present" of a dead insect wrapped in silk. Once her jaws start biting into the present, the male may safely mate with her.

The male orb-web spider approaches his oversize mate very cautiously. If he does not set up the right code of vibrations on her web, she may mistake him for an insect and eat him. The male entices the female onto a silk thread where they mate.

Courtship in newts begins when the male moves in front of the female and shows off his tail.

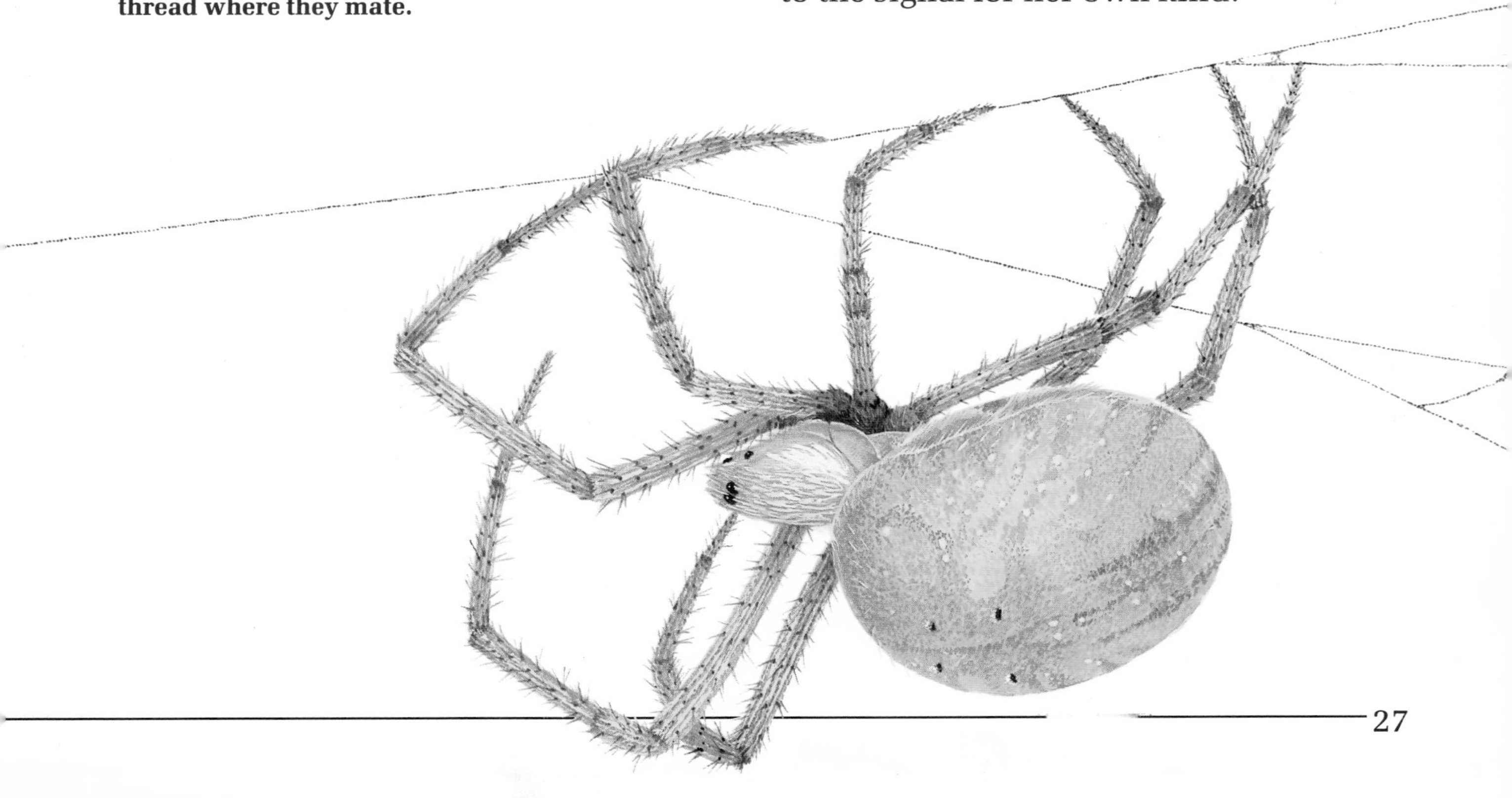

Underwater courtship

Animals that live underwater have courtship rituals, too. Sticklebacks are common, hardy, freshwater fish. In the breeding season, the male stickleback prepares a nest on the pond or stream bed. He shows off his red underside to the female stickleback in an effort to persuade her to lay her eggs in his nest.

A male newt courts his partner by waving his tail at her. In each species of newt the tail is waved at a different speed, and the female will only respond to the signal for her own kind.

COMPLEX COMMUNICATION

Most animal communication is about the transmission and understanding of a very simple message. Some animals, however, communicate in more sophisticated ways. With the aid of modern technology, scientists are discovering more about these complex signals.

Animals generally communicate by sending and receiving simple signals. But some species of animals seem able to do more than this. They use a more complicated system of signals, with different sights or sounds conveying various meanings. Sometimes they string several messages together. This more complex communication can be seen as animal language.

Talking underwater

Dolphins are intelligent animals which use sound to communicate with each other. The noises they make sound to us like a jumble of whistles, clicks, and squeaks. Scientists have tried to analyze specific sounds as a dolphin language, with different "words" for predators, prey, other dolphins, and so on. But this work is complex. It may be that dolphins are so well adapted to their environment they do not need a complex language.

Vervet monkeys use sounds to indicate different kinds of danger, but their "vocabulary" is limited.

Primates such as apes and monkeys are another class of intelligent animals. Most species of primates live in groups. They send complex messages to one another in different ways. Many forest-dwelling monkeys and apes mainly use sound to communicate with one another. Vervet monkeys from Africa use sound to warn each other of danger. If one monkey spies an eagle overhead, it will make a particular noise that means "eagle," and the other monkeys will drop to safety at ground level. But if a monkey makes the sound for "leopard," they will all quickly climb high into the trees.

Other species of primates have a similar system of warning signals, but may communicate them in a different way. Ring-tailed lemurs wave their distinctive black-and-white tails to convey visual warnings, and smear them with their scent for greater effect.

Some naturalists believe that dolphins can tell each other where to find food using sound alone.

The most intelligent species of primates, such as gorillas and chimpanzees, have developed elaborate systems of communication. These species can convey messages to each other using sight, sound, smell, touch, body language, and facial expression.

Some chimps and gorillas have been taught to use human sign language. These animals are able to use a "vocabulary" of 50 or more signs, and can even string together two or three to produce a simple "sentence." It is likely, however, that they convey many more messages to each other in the wild.

Humans are primates, too. We rely mainly on language to communicate, although gestures and facial expressions are still important to us. We are among the most communicative of all animal species, and research into human behavior in terms of threat displays, displacement activities and appeasement gestures is a fascinating area of study.

Primates spend much time and effort bringing up young, who imitate the actions of their parents.

Humans began to develop the ability to communicate through complex spoken language millions of years ago. We have evolved symbolic language and grammar as well as vocabulary far in advance of all other animals.

SPOT IT YOURSELF

You can study animals and the way they behave almost anywhere. Learn to detect creatures by the signs they leave: burrow entrances, nests, footprints in mud or snow, hair caught in wire or branches, droppings, half-eaten leaves, and discarded shells. Approach animals downwind, so your scent does not give you away. When nature-spotting, keep as still and quiet as possible.

Practical tips for nature-spotting
Wear wind- and water-proof clothing in dull colors. Polaroid glasses reduce surface reflection for seeing underwater. A lens magnifies small animals and a camping mat gives some comfort.

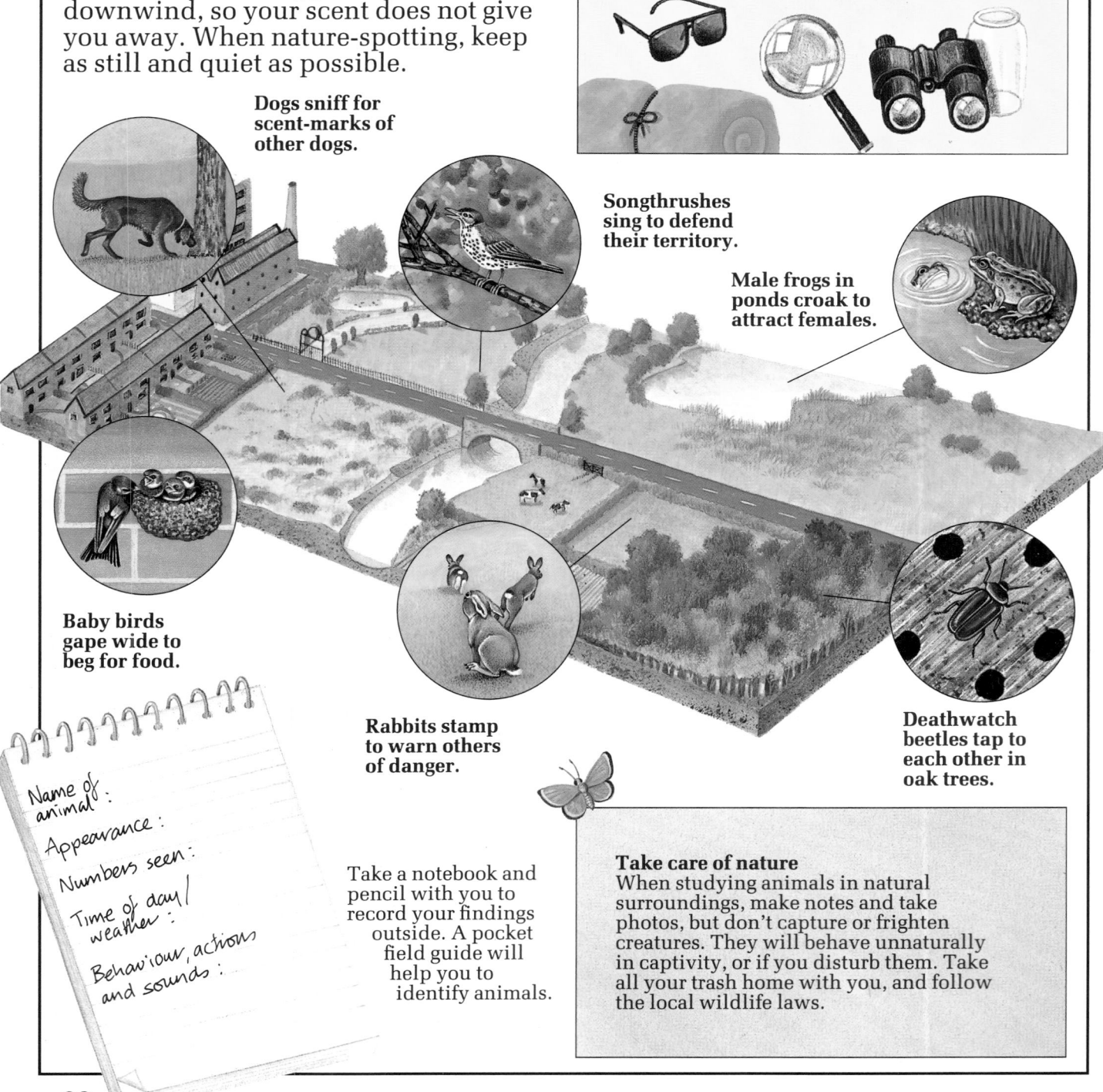

Dogs sniff for scent-marks of other dogs.

Songthrushes sing to defend their territory.

Male frogs in ponds croak to attract females.

Baby birds gape wide to beg for food.

Rabbits stamp to warn others of danger.

Deathwatch beetles tap to each other in oak trees.

Name of animal:
Appearance:
Numbers seen:
Time of day/ weather:
Behaviour, actions and sounds:

Take a notebook and pencil with you to record your findings outside. A pocket field guide will help you to identify animals.

Take care of nature
When studying animals in natural surroundings, make notes and take photos, but don't capture or frighten creatures. They will behave unnaturally in captivity, or if you disturb them. Take all your trash home with you, and follow the local wildlife laws.

GLOSSARY

Antennae Sense organs of insects and other small animals, located on the head. Antennae are sometimes called "feelers," but many animals use them for smelling as well as for touching.

Appeasement gesture Animal behavior aimed at showing submission to a more senior member of the group.

Bacteria Tiny creatures that live inside animals. Bacteria can be seen only though a microscope. Some bacteria can cause disease. Others, such as those that give off light in flashlight fish, are quite harmless.

Behavior The actions and movements of an animal, including sleeping, feeding, and courting.

Colony A group of animals of the same species that live or breed together. Sometimes, for example in honeybees, members of the colony all belong to a single family.

Grooming Keeping skin or fur clean and tidy and free from parasites.

Imprinting A kind of learning in young animals that helps them to recognize and follow their parent.

Instinct A kind of behavior that is "inbuilt" from birth, that an animal carries out without having to learn it.

Larva A young insect which has hatched from an egg, before it becomes a chrysalis or adult.

Mammal An animal that has hair (fur) and feeds its young on milk.

Mimicry Looking like something else, to avoid being seen or to avoid being attacked.

Nocturnal Active at night.

Parasite An animal that lives on or inside another and feeds on it.

Pheromone A chemical that is released by one animal to change the behavior of another.

Posture The particular way an animal stands, sits, or lies down.

Predator An animal that lives by hunting others.

Prey An animal hunted for food by a predator.

Primate The group of mammals including humans, apes, monkeys lemurs, and bushbabies.

Species A group of living things with the same characteristics, that can breed together.

Stridulation A way of making sound by rubbing together two parts of the body. Grasshoppers and locusts stridulate by rubbing their legs against their hard wing covers.

Symbiosis A relationship between two animals of different species, from which both animals benefit.

Territory An area that one animal, or a group, claims and defends.

Warning coloration Distinctive colors and patterns that warn that an animal is poisonous or that it tastes bad.

INDEX